RENEWING

WORSHIP

LITURGIES

Rites and Service Music
for Provisional Use

Evangelical Lutheran Church in America
Published by Augsburg Fortress

RENEWING WORSHIP LITURGIES

Also available:

Renewing Worship Liturgies Accompaniment Edition AFP 0-8066-7026-6

Study and leader editions of materials in *Renewing Worship Liturgies*:
Holy Communion and Related Rites: Renewing Worship, vol. 6
AFP 0-8066-7006-1
Holy Baptism and Related Rites: Renewing Worship, vol. 3
AFP 0-8066-7002-9
Life Passages: Marriage, Healing, Funeral: Renewing Worship, vol. 4
AFP 0-8066-7004-5

This resource has been prepared by the Evangelical Lutheran Church in America for provisional use.

Manufactured in the U.S.A.   ISBN 0-8066-7025-8

06   05   04   2   3

Contents

4   Preface

7   Holy Communion

Shape of the Rite   7
Provisional Setting A   10
Provisional Setting B   24

38   Word and Thanksgiving

Shape of the Rite   38
Word and Thanksgiving   39

44   Holy Baptism

Shape of the Rite   44
Holy Baptism   45

51   Service Music

Contents   51
Service Music   R312–R366

94   Acknowledgments

95   Indexes

Preface

In the years since the publication of *Lutheran Book of Worship* in 1978, the pace of change both within the church and beyond has quickened. The past three decades have seen not only areas of growing ecumenical consensus but also a deepened focus on the church's mission to the world. The church has embraced broadened understandings of culture, increasing musical diversity, changes in the usage of language, a renewed understanding of the central pattern of Christian worship, and an explosion of electronic media and technologies. These shifts have had a profound effect on the weekly assembly gathered around word and sacrament. The present situation calls for a renewal of worship and of common resources for worship, a renewal grounded in the treasures of the church's history while open to the possibilities of the future.

RENEWING WORSHIP

Renewing Worship is a response to these emerging changes in the life of the church and the world. This initiative, endorsed by the Church Council of the Evangelical Lutheran Church in America (ELCA) and carried out in partnership by the ELCA Division for Congregational Ministries and the Publishing House of the ELCA (Augsburg Fortress), has been underway since 2000. One part of the Renewing Worship initiative is a series of provisional resources intended to address the various liturgical and musical needs of the church, looking toward the next generation of primary worship resources. These resources have been developed through a process involving a broad spectrum of laypeople, pastors, teachers, and musicians. This booklet is a sampling of some of the liturgies and musical settings that have been developed. Complete versions of the provisional resources are published in a number of volumes available from Augsburg Fortress. Much of the same material is also available in electronic form delivered via the Internet (www.renewingworship.org).

It is vital that those who use these provisional resources respond with evaluations. Of the texts and music presented, what works well? What still needs tinkering? What do you think is missing or needs rethinking? Complete evaluation forms are found in each of the main study volumes of Renewing Worship resources. In addition, the Renewing Worship Web site (www.renewingworship.org) provides a way for users to submit evaluations. Such response by congregations and worship leaders will be a great help as a comprehensive proposal for new primary worship resources designed to succeed *Lutheran Book of Worship* is brought to completion.

RENEWING WORSHIP LITURGIES

This booklet, *Renewing Worship Liturgies*, contains abridged forms of provisional liturgies from two volumes, *Holy Communion and Related Rites* (Renewing Worship, vol. 6) and *Holy Baptism and Related Rites* (Renewing Worship, vol. 3). They are collected here in order to make it easier for congregations to use them in weekly worship. In these pages you will find the Shape of the Rite for the communion and baptism liturgies, meant to help users see the broad outline of these rites. Two new musical settings of the communion liturgy are provided, both using the same texts. These settings include music for the acclamations that are central to the word and meal parts of the liturgy. A separate Service Music section contains settings of canticles and acclamations for other parts of the liturgy, as well as alternatives to the musical settings printed within the liturgies. For those occasions when a full liturgy of word and sacrament is not celebrated, a Service of Word and Thanksgiving provides a non-eucharistic ending to the primary communion liturgy.

The liturgy for baptism provided here is intended for use within the communion liturgy. Typically the baptismal liturgy follows the hymn of the day, in place of the creed. The remembrance of baptism is not used at the beginning of the gathering rite when baptism takes place during the liturgy. The baptismal liturgy may also replace the remembrance of baptism in the gathering rite, in which case the creed is not used later in the service.

MUSIC OF THE LITURGIES

It needs to be emphasized that the musical settings presented here are preliminary steps toward a new primary resource. Most of the music in this volume is new to Lutherans; a longer-term resource will blend familiar with new. Some of the approaches to layout, such as the separate service music section, may or may not be carried forward, depending in large part on evaluations that are submitted. Another concept being tested is providing varied accompaniment styles for a given melody; both musical settings illustrate this strategy. Varied musical accompaniments are provided in *Renewing Worship Liturgies* Accompaniment Edition.

In addition to music for Holy Communion and Word and Thanksgiving, some samples of musical acclamations for baptism, remembrance of baptism, marriage, healing, and funeral rites are provided in the service music section. Additional settings are available for download through www.renewingworship.org.

PATTERNS AND WORDS FOR WORSHIP

In addition to trying out new musical settings, these provisional resources bring the opportunity to evaluate some proposed revisions to patterns and words for worship. The gathering portion of the communion liturgy is opened up, with alternate forms for baptismal remembrance providing one way of beginning the worship. This idea of flexibility within the structure is continued as different texts are offered to conclude the first and second readings. The creeds and the beginning of the great thanksgiving make use of wording shared among many English-speaking Christians, wording that varies slightly in places from that used in *Lutheran Book of Worship*. The sending section invites responses to some new texts. Additional supplemental texts are available in the study volumes and on the Web site. Overall, however, the shape of the liturgy should be familiar to those who have used *LBW* and *WOV*.

Another change in the presentation of the rites that is being tested here is the omission of instructions about posture (standing, sitting, kneeling). Generally, it is customary for the assembly to stand for the gathering rite, the acclamation and proclamation of the gospel, the hymn of the day through the peace, the great thanksgiving, and the communion prayer through the sending. Kneeling is customary in many places at the prayer of confession and, in some places, also at the prayer of the day and the prayers of intercession (except during Easter). The needs and circumstances of particular contexts vary widely, however, and so instructions about posture have been omitted in these provisional resources. Careful worship leadership will make verbal announcements about posture unnecessary in most cases.

Much thought and spirited discussion has gone into the crafting of these resources. Even so, they are simply one step along the way. Your responses and constructive criticism will help carry the church to the next step. Finally, though, Renewing Worship is about more than just resources. It is about the Holy Spirit renewing the worship of God in the church as it carries out Christ's mission in a new day.

HOLY COMMUNION
Shape of the Rite

At the heart of Christian worship is Jesus Christ, given by God through concrete and specific means. Through *baptism* God makes a people one body in Christ. In the *assembly* God gathers the people by the Holy Spirit. God's *word* is the message of Christ proclaimed in scripture reading, preaching, prayer, and singing. In the *meal* of communion God gives us Christ's very self in bread and wine. God then sends us to participate in Christ's mission in all the world.

The common shape of Christian worship has its roots in the scriptures. The story of the road to Emmaus in Luke 24 suggests a pattern that has been reflected in the church's worship since its earliest days. The story takes place on the first day of the week. A gathering of Jesus and two disciples focuses on the word, as the risen Christ explains the scriptures beginning with Moses and the prophets. In the meal that follows, the disciples recognize Jesus in the breaking of the bread. This recognition sends them out to share the news with others. A similar pattern is described in the book of Acts: the Christian community gathered on the first day of the week and devoted themselves to the apostles' teaching, to fellowship, to the breaking of bread, and to prayer.

Worship in word and sacrament continues to follow the simple pattern of gathering, word, meal, and sending, even though a variety of forms and styles may mark its practice. In fact, rich diversity of styles and openness to the ways of many peoples and nations can underscore how the central gifts of God unite us into one people in Christ. Worship in word and sacrament may be simple or it may be complex. But simplicity will not leave out the central things and complexity will not overshadow them.

Because worship takes place in contemporary settings, it is always current and new. At this very time, right now, the people meet the crucified and risen Christ, who baptizes into community, proclaims the word, feeds and nourishes with his body and blood, and sends the church to continue to be the body of Christ in the world.

Because worship is centered in word and sacrament, it always also extends beyond this time and place. Worship continues the story of all who have gone before us in faith, and so it always extends the wealth handed down from all those who have gathered and baptized, listened and shared the meal, and been sent to serve. Worship also connects the people of God across the world in the same word and sacrament and mission.

Worship in word and sacrament is God's gift to the church. The simple shape of the liturgy encourages local freedom to flower from a deep and faithful common ground. The life-giving gifts of God flow from the Holy Spirit who brings us to faith. They draw us into participation in the crucified and risen Christ. They show forth God's love for the world and make us part of that love. The central gifts of word and sacrament gather us into the very life of the triune God, the God who gives life to the world.

HOLY COMMUNION
Shape of the Rite

| GATHERING | *The Holy Spirit gathers us in unity on the first day of the week, the day of Christ's resurrection.* |

Remembrance of Baptism — *We remember our baptism . . .*

   Confession and Forgiveness — *. . . as we confess our need of God's mercy and hear the word of forgiveness,*
   OR
   Thanksgiving for Baptism — *. . . as we give thanks for God's mercy in the saving waters.*

Gathering Song — *We enter singing.*

   Hymn, Song, Psalm — *We draw from a rich treasury of song.*
   AND/OR
   Kyrie — *We pray for God's mercy to fill the church and the world.*
   AND/OR
   Canticle of Praise — *We sing the praise of God's glory revealed in Jesus Christ.*

Greeting — *The presiding minister and the assembly greet each other in the name of the triune God.*

Prayer of the Day — *The presiding minister leads the gathered assembly in prayer.*

WORD
God speaks to us in scriptures read, sung, and preached.

First Reading — *We listen to a scripture reading, most often from the Old Testament.*

Psalm — *We sing a psalm in response to the first reading.*

Second Reading — *We listen to a scripture reading, most often from the New Testament letters.*

Gospel Acclamation — *Singing, we welcome the gospel.*

Gospel — *We listen to a reading from one of the four gospels.*

Sermon — *We encounter the living word of God in the preaching.*

Hymn of the Day — *We proclaim the word of God in song.*

Creed — *With the baptized of every time and place we profess the faith.*

Prayers of Intercession — *We pray for the whole world.*

Peace — *At the close of the prayers, we greet one another with the peace of Christ.*

MEAL

God feeds us with the presence of Jesus Christ.

Gathering of Gifts	*We gather gifts for those in need and the church's mission.*
Setting the Table	*Singing, we bring these gifts and set the table with bread and wine.*
Great Thanksgiving	*We thank and praise God, proclaiming Jesus Christ, praying for the Spirit, and concluding with the prayer Jesus taught.*
Dialog and Thanksgiving	*Opening our hearts to God, we begin the thanksgiving.*
Holy, Holy, Holy	*With the whole creation we join the angels' song.*
Thanksgiving	*Proclaiming and giving thanks for all God has done,*
Words of Institution	*we hear the promise of Jesus' gift through this meal.*
Remembrance and Acclamation	*We remember and acclaim the crucified and risen Christ.*
Prayer for the Holy Spirit	*We pray that the Holy Spirit come upon us and this meal.*
Final Praise and Amen	*We say Yes to this thanksgiving and to Christ among us.*
Lord's Prayer	*Empowered by the Spirit, we pray as Jesus taught us.*
OR	
Dialog and Thanksgiving	*Opening our hearts to God, we begin the thanksgiving.*
Holy, Holy, Holy	*With the whole creation we join the angels' song.*
Words of Institution	*We hear the promise of Jesus' gift through this meal.*
Lord's Prayer	*Empowered by the Spirit, we pray as Jesus taught us.*
Communion	*Christ's body and blood nourishes faith, forgives sin, and forms us as living witnesses to God's promise of unity, justice, and peace.*
Communion Song	*We sing as the bread is broken, as the meal is shared, as the ministers commune.*
Communion Prayer	*Thanking God for these gifts, we ask God to send us in witness to the world.*

SENDING

God blesses us and sends us in mission to the world.

Sending of Communion Ministers	*We send ministers of communion to take the sacrament to the absent.*
Blessing	*We receive the blessing of the triune God.*
Sending Song	*Singing, we go out from the assembly as God's people in mission.*
Sending	*God sends us to live as Christ's body in the world.*

Central elements of the liturgy are noted in bold letters; other elements support and reveal the essential shape of Christian worship.

HOLY COMMUNION
Provisional Setting A

GATHERING

Instrumental or vocal music or rehearsal of congregational song may take place while the assembly is gathering. An announcement of the day may be made, along with any brief comments about the day's worship.

The remembrance of baptism may precede gathering song. One of the following or another appropriate form may be used. If possible, the ministers (and the assembly) gather at the font.

I   REMEMBRANCE OF BAPTISM
Confession and Forgiveness

All may make the sign of the cross in remembrance of baptism as the presiding minister begins:

A

Trusting in the word of life
given in baptism,
we are gathered in the name
of the Father, and of the ✝ Son,
and of the Holy Spirit.
Amen.

B

Blessed be God,
who gives us life with all of creation,
joins us to the saving death of ✝ Christ,
and raises us to new life by the Holy Spirit.
Blessed be the Holy Trinity.
Blessed be God forever.

The presiding minister may lead a prayer of preparation:
God of all mercy and consolation,
come to the aid of your people,
turning us from our sin to live for you alone.
Give us the power of your Holy Spirit
that we may confess our sins,
receive your forgiveness,
and grow into the fullness of your Son,
Jesus Christ our Lord.
Amen.

An assisting minister may invite the assembly into the confession:

God so loved the world
that while we were yet sinners
Jesus Christ was given to die for us.
Through the power of the Holy Spirit
God promises to heal us and forgive us.
Let us confess our sin
in the presence of God and of one another.

Silence is kept for reflection and self-examination.

The presiding minister leads a prayer of confession:

A

Gracious God,
**have mercy on us.
In your compassion
forgive us our sins,
known and unknown,
things done and things left undone.
Uphold us by your Spirit
so that we may live and serve you
in newness of life,
to the honor and glory
of your holy name;
through Jesus Christ our Lord.
Amen.**

B

Merciful God,
**we have sinned against you
in thought, word, and deed,
and are not worthy
to be called your children.
Have mercy on us
and turn us from our sinful ways.
Bring us back to you
as those who once were dead
but now have life,
through our Savior Jesus Christ.
Amen.**

The presiding minister announces God's forgiveness:

A

Almighty God looks upon us with mercy
and by water and the word joins us
to the saving death of Jesus Christ.
Through the Holy Spirit
God raises us with Christ to new life.
I therefore declare to you
the entire forgiveness of all your sins,
in the name of the Father,
and of the ✝ Son,
and of the Holy Spirit.
Amen.

B

Almighty God have mercy on you,
forgive you all your sins
through our Lord Jesus Christ,
strengthen you in all goodness,
and by the power of the Holy Spirit
keep you in eternal life.
Amen.

The liturgy may continue with gathering song.

II REMEMBRANCE OF BAPTISM
Thanksgiving for Baptism

All may make the sign of the cross in remembrance of baptism as the presiding minister begins:

A	B
Trusting in the word of life	Blessed be God,
given in baptism,	who gives us life with all of creation,
we are gathered in the name	joins us to the saving death of ✝ Christ,
of the Father, and of the ✝ Son,	and raises us to new life by the Holy Spirit.
and of the Holy Spirit.	Blessed be the Holy Trinity.
Amen.	**Blessed be God forever.**

The assisting minister invites the assembly into the remembrance of baptism:
When we were joined to Christ in the waters of baptism,
we were clothed with God's mercy and forgiveness.
Together let us remember our baptism.

Water may be poured into the font as the presiding minister gives thanks:
The Lord be with you.
And also with you.

Let us give thanks to the Lord our God.
It is right to give our thanks and praise.

We give you thanks, O God, for in the beginning your Spirit brooded over the waters and you created the world by your Word, calling forth life in which you took delight. You led Israel safely through the Red Sea into the land of promise, and in the waters of the Jordan, you proclaimed Jesus your beloved one. By water and the Spirit you adopted us as your daughters and sons, making us heirs of the promise and servants of God. Through this water remind us of our baptism. Shower us with your Spirit, that your forgiveness, grace, and love may be renewed in our lives. To you be given honor and praise through Jesus Christ our Lord in the unity of the Holy Spirit, now and forever.
Amen.

The water may be sprinkled over the people or they may be invited to use it to sign them-
selves with the cross. During this time gathering song may be sung. Hymns and songs related
to baptism are especially appropriate. R347–R355 ▶

The liturgy continues with the greeting and the prayer of the day.

GATHERING SONG

One or more of the following may be sung as the assembly gathers:

Hymn, Song, Psalm

Kyrie
When a Kyrie is sung, one of the following or another appropriate form may be used.

Kyrie (Litany)	R312–R313 ▸
Kyrie (Threefold, Sixfold, or Ninefold)	R314–R317 ▸
Holy God (Trisagion)	R318–R319 ▸

Canticle of Praise
When a canticle of praise is sung, one of the following or another appropriate song may be used.

Glory to God	R320–R322 ▸
This Is the Feast	R323–R324 ▸

GREETING

The presiding minister and the assembly greet each other:
The grace of our Lord Jesus Christ, the love of God,
and the communion of the Holy Spirit be with you all.
And also with you.

PRAYER OF THE DAY

The presiding minister prays the prayer of the day:
Let us pray.

A brief silence is kept before the prayer. After the prayer, the assembly responds:
Amen.

WORD

An announcement of the day may be made, along with any brief comments about the day's liturgy.

FIRST READING

An assisting minister proclaims the reading. The reading may be concluded:

A

Holy wisdom, holy word.
Thanks be to God.

B

The word of the Lord.
Thanks be to God.

PSALM *The psalm for the day is sung.*

SECOND READING

An assisting minister proclaims the reading. The reading may be concluded:

A

Holy wisdom, holy word.
Thanks be to God.

B

The word of the Lord.
Thanks be to God.

GOSPEL ACCLAMATION

The assembly welcomes the gospel. The verse of the day (R325) or the following verse may be sung.
The assembly or the choir may sing another alleluia, with or without verse, in place of this one.

R301   R325–R329 ▶

Al - le - lu - ia,   al - le - lu - ia.

Al - le - lu - ia,   al - le - lu - ia.

Your words are sweet to our taste,

sweet-er than hon - ey to our mouth. Al - le -

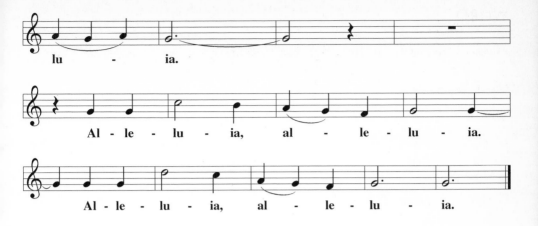

lu - ia.

Al - le - lu - ia, al - le - lu - ia.

Al - le - lu - ia, al - le - lu - ia.

During Lent, the verse of the day, the following verse, or another seasonal acclamation may be sung.

R302   R330 ▶

Let your stead - fast love come to us, O Lord;

save us as you prom - ised, for we trust your word.

GOSPEL

The gospel is announced.
The holy gospel according to _____, the _____ chapter.
Glory to you, O Lord.

The gospel is proclaimed. The reading concludes:
The gospel of the Lord.
Praise to you, O Christ.

SERMON

Silence for reflection follows.

HYMN OF THE DAY

The assembly proclaims the word of God in song.

CREED

The assembly may profess the Nicene Creed or the Apostles Creed. The Nicene Creed is especially appropriate during Christmas, Easter, and on festival days; the Apostles Creed during Lent.

Nicene Creed

We believe in one God,
   the Father, the Almighty,
   maker of heaven and earth,
   of all that is, seen and unseen.

We believe in one Lord, Jesus Christ,
   the only Son of God,
   eternally begotten of the Father,
   God from God, Light from Light,
   true God from true God,
   begotten, not made,
   of one Being with the Father;
   through him all things were made.
   For us and for our salvation
      he came down from heaven,
      was incarnate of the Holy Spirit and the virgin Mary
      and became truly human.
      For our sake he was crucified under Pontius Pilate;
      he suffered death and was buried.
      On the third day he rose again
      in accordance with the scriptures;
      he ascended into heaven
      and is seated at the right hand of the Father.
      He will come again in glory to judge the living and the dead,
      and his kingdom will have no end.

We believe in the Holy Spirit, the Lord, the giver of life,
   who proceeds from the Father and the Son,*
   who with the Father and the Son is worshiped and glorified,
   who has spoken through the prophets.
   We believe in one holy catholic and apostolic church.
   We acknowledge one baptism for the forgiveness of sins.
   We look for the resurrection of the dead,
      and the life of the world to come. Amen.

The phrase "and the Son" does not appear in the ancient, ecumenical version of the creed.

Apostles Creed

I believe in God, the Father almighty,
    creator of heaven and earth.

I believe in Jesus Christ, God's only Son, our Lord,
    who was conceived by the Holy Spirit,
    born of the virgin Mary,
    suffered under Pontius Pilate,
    was crucified, died, and was buried;
    he descended to the dead.
    On the third day he rose again;
    he ascended into heaven,
    he is seated at the right hand of the Father,
    and he will come to judge the living and the dead.

I believe in the Holy Spirit,
    the holy catholic church,
    the communion of saints,
    the forgiveness of sins,
    the resurrection of the body,
    and the life everlasting. Amen.

PRAYERS OF INTERCESSION

The prayers are crafted locally for each occasion using this pattern or another appropriate form.

An assisting minister invites the assembly into prayer with these or similar words:
With the whole people of God in Christ Jesus, let us pray for the church, those in need, and all of God's creation.

Prayers reflect the wideness of God's mercy for the whole world: for the church universal and its ministry; for creation and its right use; for peace and justice in the world, the nations and those in authority, the community and those who govern; for the poor and oppressed, the sick, the bereaved, the lonely, all who suffer in body, mind, or spirit; for the congregation, and special concerns. The congregation may be invited to offer other petitions. The assisting minister gives thanks for the faithful departed, especially for those who recently have died.

Each portion of the prayers concludes with these or similar words:

A	B	R331 ►
Lord, in your mercy,	Hear us, O God;	
hear our prayer.	**your mercy is great.**	

The presiding minister concludes the prayers with these or similar words:
Into your hands, gracious God, we commend all for whom we pray,
trusting in your mercy; through Jesus Christ our Savior.
Amen.

PEACE

The presiding minister and the assembly greet each other in the peace of the risen Christ:

A

Peace be with you all.

And also with you.

B

The peace of Christ be with you always.

And also with you.

The ministers and the assembly may greet one another with a gesture of Christ's peace, and may say these or similar words: Peace be with you.

MEAL

GATHERING OF GIFTS

Gifts may be gathered for those in need and for the mission of the church.

SETTING THE TABLE

The table of the eucharistic meal is prepared. "Let the vineyards be fruitful" (R332–R333), "Create in me a clean heart" (R334), or another appropriate canticle, song, or hymn may be sung as bread, wine, money, and other gifts are brought to the table. A brief prayer may follow.

GREAT THANKSGIVING

The presiding minister greets the assembly and invites all present to give thanks:

The Lord be with you. **And al - so with you.**

Lift up your hearts. **We lift them to the Lord.**

Let us give thanks to the Lord our God.

It is right to give our thanks and praise.

The presiding minister continues with an initial thanksgiving:

It is indeed right, our duty and our joy . . .
(Here the minister may use the initial thanksgiving appointed for the day or season, concluding:)
. . . join their unending hymn:

Ho - ly, ho - ly, ho - ly Lord,
God of pow - er and might,
heav-en and earth are full of your glo - ry.
Ho - san - na in the high - est,
ho - san - na in the high - est.
Bless - ed is he who comes in the name of the Lord.
Ho - san - na in the high - est, ho -
san - na in the high - est.

*Sing either note.

The presiding minister continues the thanksgiving, using one of the following forms.

A *The presiding minister leads a prayer of thanksgiving at table. The following acclamation may be sung as part of the prayer:*

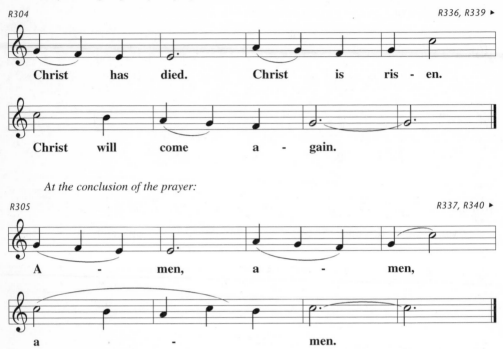

At the conclusion of the prayer:

The Lord's Prayer concludes the great thanksgiving:

Gathered into one by the Holy Spirit, let us pray as Jesus taught us:

A	B

Our Father in heaven,
     hallowed be your name,
     your kingdom come,
     your will be done,
          on earth as in heaven.
Give us today our daily bread.
Forgive us our sins
     as we forgive those
          who sin against us.
Save us from the time of trial
     and deliver us from evil.
For the kingdom, the power,
     and the glory are yours,
     now and forever. Amen.
	Our Father, who art in heaven,
	     hallowed be thy name,
	     thy kingdom come,
	     thy will be done,
	          on earth as it is in heaven.
	Give us this day our daily bread;
	and forgive us our trespasses,
	     as we forgive those
	          who trespass against us;
	and lead us not into temptation,
	     but deliver us from evil.
	For thine is the kingdom,
	     and the power, and the glory,
	     forever and ever. Amen.

The presiding minister proclaims the promise of Jesus' gift through this meal, using the words of institution.

The Lord's Prayer concludes the great thanksgiving. This form or one of those on page 20 may be used.

Gathered into one by the Ho-ly Spir-it, let us pray as Je-sus taught us:

Our Fa-ther in heav-en, hal-lowed be your name,

your king-dom come, your will be done, on earth as in

heav-en. Give us to-day our dai-ly bread.

For-give us our sins as we for-give those who sin a-gainst us.

Save us from the time of tri-al and de-liv-er us from e-vil.

For the king-dom, the pow'r, and the glo-ry are yours,

now and for-ev-er. A-men.

COMMUNION

The presiding minister may raise the bread and cup and address the assembly with these or similar words:

A	B
Holy things for holy people.	The gifts of God for the people of God.
One is holy, one is Lord,	**Thanks be to God.**
Jesus Christ, to the glory of God.

The assisting minister may conclude the invitation to the meal:
Taste and see that the Lord is good.

The bread may be broken for the communion.

When giving the bread and cup, the communion ministers say:
The body of Christ, given for you. The blood of Christ, shed for you.
and the communicant may respond, Amen.

The ministers commune either after or before the communion of the assembly.

Communion Song
Assembly song and other music may accompany the breaking of bread and the communion of the people, and may begin with "Lamb of God."   R341–R343 ▸

At the conclusion of the communion, "Now, Lord, you let your servant go" or another appropriate song may be sung as the table is cleared.   R344–R346 ▸

Communion Prayer
An assisting minister leads one of these or a similar prayer:
Let us pray.

A	B
We give you thanks, almighty God,	O God, we give you thanks
that you have refreshed us	that you have set before us this feast,
through the healing power	the body and blood of your Son.
of this gift of life.	By your Spirit
In your mercy	strengthen us to serve all in want
strengthen us through this gift	and to give ourselves away
in faith toward you	as bread for the hungry,
and in fervent love toward one another;	through Jesus Christ our Lord.
for the sake of Jesus Christ our Lord.	**Amen.**
Amen.

SENDING

SENDING OF COMMUNION MINISTERS

Communion ministers may be sent to bring the sacrament to those who are absent. The presiding minister may lead a prayer of sending.

Brief announcements related to the assembly's mission in the world may be made.

BLESSING

The presiding minister blesses the assembly with one of these or another appropriate blessing:

A

Holy Eternal Majesty,
Holy Incarnate Word,
Holy Abiding Spirit,
one God, ✝ bless you
now and forever.
Amen.

B

The Lord bless you
and keep you.
The Lord's face shine on you
with grace and mercy.
The Lord look upon you
with favor
and ✝ give you peace.
Amen.

C

Almighty God,
Father, ✝ Son,
and Holy Spirit,
bless you
now and forever.
Amen.

SENDING SONG

If "Now, Lord, you let your servant go" was not sung at the end of the communion, it may be sung here, or another sending song may be sung. The ministers may move to the door.

SENDING

The assisting minister sends the assembly forth with these or similar words:

A

Go in peace.
Share the good news.
Thanks be to God.

B

Go in peace.
Remember the poor.
Thanks be to God.

C

Go in peace.
Serve the Lord.
Thanks be to God.

HOLY COMMUNION
Provisional Setting B

GATHERING

Instrumental or vocal music or rehearsal of congregational song may take place while the assembly is gathering. An announcement of the day may be made, along with any brief comments about the day's worship.

The remembrance of baptism may precede gathering song. One of the following or another appropriate form may be used. If possible, the ministers (and the assembly) gather at the font.

I REMEMBRANCE OF BAPTISM
Confession and Forgiveness

All may make the sign of the cross in remembrance of baptism as the presiding minister begins:

A	B
Trusting in the word of life	Blessed be God,
given in baptism,	who gives us life with all of creation,
we are gathered in the name	joins us to the saving death of ✝ Christ,
of the Father, and of the ✝ Son,	and raises us to new life by the Holy Spirit.
and of the Holy Spirit.	Blessed be the Holy Trinity.
Amen.	**Blessed be God forever.**

The presiding minister may lead a prayer of preparation:
God of all mercy and consolation,
come to the aid of your people,
turning us from our sin to live for you alone.
Give us the power of your Holy Spirit
that we may confess our sins,
receive your forgiveness,
and grow into the fullness of your Son,
Jesus Christ our Lord.
Amen.

An assisting minister may invite the assembly into the confession:

God so loved the world
that while we were yet sinners
Jesus Christ was given to die for us.
Through the power of the Holy Spirit
God promises to heal us and forgive us.
Let us confess our sin
in the presence of God and of one another.
Silence is kept for reflection and self-examination.

The presiding minister leads a prayer of confession:

A

Gracious God,
have mercy on us.
In your compassion
forgive us our sins,
known and unknown,
things done and things left undone.
Uphold us by your Spirit
so that we may live and serve you
in newness of life,
to the honor and glory
of your holy name;
through Jesus Christ our Lord.
Amen.

B

Merciful God,
we have sinned against you
in thought, word, and deed,
and are not worthy
to be called your children.
Have mercy on us
and turn us from our sinful ways.
Bring us back to you
as those who once were dead
but now have life,
through our Savior Jesus Christ.
Amen.

The presiding minister announces God's forgiveness:

A

Almighty God looks upon us with mercy
and by water and the word joins us
to the saving death of Jesus Christ.
Through the Holy Spirit
God raises us with Christ to new life.
I therefore declare to you
the entire forgiveness of all your sins,
in the name of the Father,
and of the ✠ Son,
and of the Holy Spirit.
Amen.

B

Almighty God have mercy on you,
forgive you all your sins
through our Lord Jesus Christ,
strengthen you in all goodness,
and by the power of the Holy Spirit
keep you in eternal life.
Amen.

The liturgy may continue with gathering song.

II REMEMBRANCE OF BAPTISM
Thanksgiving for Baptism

All may make the sign of the cross in remembrance of baptism as the presiding minister begins:

A	B
Trusting in the word of life	Blessed be God,
given in baptism,	who gives us life with all of creation,
we are gathered in the name	joins us to the saving death of ✠ Christ,
of the Father, and of the ✠ Son,	and raises us to new life by the Holy Spirit.
and of the Holy Spirit.	Blessed be the Holy Trinity.
Amen.	**Blessed be God forever.**

The assisting minister invites the assembly into the remembrance of baptism:
When we were joined to Christ in the waters of baptism,
we were clothed with God's mercy and forgiveness.
Together let us remember our baptism.

Water may be poured into the font as the presiding minister gives thanks:
The Lord be with you.
And also with you.

Let us give thanks to the Lord our God.
It is right to give our thanks and praise.

We give you thanks, O God, for in the beginning your Spirit brooded over the
waters and you created the world by your Word, calling forth life in which you took
delight. You led Israel safely through the Red Sea into the land of promise, and in
the waters of the Jordan, you proclaimed Jesus your beloved one. By water and the
Spirit you adopted us as your daughters and sons, making us heirs of the promise
and servants of God. Through this water remind us of our baptism. Shower us with
your Spirit, that your forgiveness, grace, and love may be renewed in our lives. To
you be given honor and praise through Jesus Christ our Lord in the unity of the
Holy Spirit, now and forever.
Amen.

The water may be sprinkled over the people or they may be invited to use it to sign them-
selves with the cross. During this time gathering song may be sung. Hymns and songs related
to baptism are especially appropriate. R347–R355 ▶

The liturgy continues with the greeting and the prayer of the day.

GATHERING SONG

One or more of the following may be sung as the assembly gathers:

Hymn, Song, Psalm

Kyrie
When a Kyrie is sung, one of the following or another appropriate form may be used.

Kyrie (Litany)	*R312–R313* ▶
Kyrie (Threefold, Sixfold, or Ninefold)	*R314–R317* ▶
Holy God (Trisagion)	*R318–R319* ▶

Canticle of Praise
When a canticle of praise is sung, one of the following or another appropriate song may be used.

Glory to God	*R320–R322* ▶
This Is the Feast	*R323–R324* ▶

GREETING

The presiding minister and the assembly greet each other:
The grace of our Lord Jesus Christ, the love of God,
and the communion of the Holy Spirit be with you all.
And also with you.

PRAYER OF THE DAY

The presiding minister prays the prayer of the day:
Let us pray.

A brief silence is kept before the prayer. After the prayer, the assembly responds:
Amen.

WORD

An announcement of the day may be made, along with any brief comments about the day's liturgy.

FIRST READING

An assisting minister proclaims the reading. The reading may be concluded:

A   B

Holy wisdom, holy word.   The word of the Lord.

Thanks be to God.   **Thanks be to God.**

PSALM *The psalm for the day is sung.*

SECOND READING

An assisting minister proclaims the reading. The reading may be concluded:

A   B

Holy wisdom, holy word.   The word of the Lord.

Thanks be to God.   **Thanks be to God.**

GOSPEL ACCLAMATION

The assembly welcomes the gospel. The verse of the day (R327) or the following verse may be sung.
The assembly or the choir may sing another alleluia, with or without verse, in place of this one.

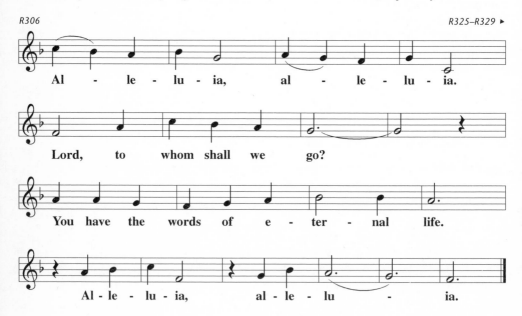

R306   R325–R329 ▶

Al - le - lu - ia, al - le - lu - ia.
Lord, to whom shall we go?
You have the words of e - ter - nal life.
Al - le - lu - ia, al - le - lu - ia.

During Lent, the verse of the day, the following verse, or another seasonal acclamation may be sung.

R307

R330 ▶

Let your stead - fast love come to us, O Lord;

Save us as you prom - ised, for we trust your word;

save us as you prom - ised, for we trust your word.

GOSPEL

The gospel is announced.
The holy gospel according to _____, the _____ chapter.
Glory to you, O Lord.

The gospel is proclaimed. The reading concludes:
The gospel of the Lord.
Praise to you, O Christ.

SERMON

Silence for reflection follows.

HYMN OF THE DAY

The assembly proclaims the word of God in song.

CREED

The assembly may profess the Nicene Creed or the Apostles Creed. The Nicene Creed is especially appropriate during Christmas, Easter, and on festival days; the Apostles Creed during Lent.

Nicene Creed

We believe in one God,
   the Father, the Almighty,
   maker of heaven and earth,
   of all that is, seen and unseen.

We believe in one Lord, Jesus Christ,
   the only Son of God,
   eternally begotten of the Father,
   God from God, Light from Light,
   true God from true God,
   begotten, not made,
   of one Being with the Father;
   through him all things were made.
   For us and for our salvation
      he came down from heaven,
      was incarnate of the Holy Spirit and the virgin Mary
      and became truly human.
      For our sake he was crucified under Pontius Pilate;
      he suffered death and was buried.
      On the third day he rose again
      in accordance with the scriptures;
      he ascended into heaven
      and is seated at the right hand of the Father.
      He will come again in glory to judge the living and the dead,
      and his kingdom will have no end.

We believe in the Holy Spirit, the Lord, the giver of life,
   who proceeds from the Father and the Son,*
   who with the Father and the Son is worshiped and glorified,
   who has spoken through the prophets.
   We believe in one holy catholic and apostolic church.
   We acknowledge one baptism for the forgiveness of sins.
   We look for the resurrection of the dead,
      and the life of the world to come. Amen.

The phrase "and the Son" does not appear in the ancient, ecumenical version of the creed.

Apostles Creed

I believe in God, the Father almighty,
   creator of heaven and earth.

I believe in Jesus Christ, God's only Son, our Lord,
   who was conceived by the Holy Spirit,
   born of the virgin Mary,
   suffered under Pontius Pilate,
   was crucified, died, and was buried;
   he descended to the dead.
   On the third day he rose again;
   he ascended into heaven,
   he is seated at the right hand of the Father,
   and he will come to judge the living and the dead.

I believe in the Holy Spirit,
   the holy catholic church,
   the communion of saints,
   the forgiveness of sins,
   the resurrection of the body,
   and the life everlasting. Amen.

PRAYERS OF INTERCESSION

The prayers are crafted locally for each occasion using this pattern or another appropriate form.

An assisting minister invites the assembly into prayer with these or similar words:
With the whole people of God in Christ Jesus, let us pray for the church, those in need, and all of God's creation.

Prayers reflect the wideness of God's mercy for the whole world: for the church universal and its ministry; for creation and its right use; for peace and justice in the world, the nations and those in authority, the community and those who govern; for the poor and oppressed, the sick, the bereaved, the lonely, all who suffer in body, mind, or spirit; for the congregation, and special concerns. The congregation may be invited to offer other petitions. The assisting minister gives thanks for the faithful departed, especially for those who recently have died.

Each portion of the prayers concludes with these or similar words:

A	B	R331 ▶
Lord, in your mercy,	Hear us, O God;	
hear our prayer.	**your mercy is great.**	

The presiding minister concludes the prayers with these or similar words:
Into your hands, gracious God, we commend all for whom we pray,
trusting in your mercy; through Jesus Christ our Savior.
Amen.

PEACE

The presiding minister and the assembly greet each other in the peace of the risen Christ:

A

Peace be with you all.

And also with you.

B

The peace of Christ be with you always.

And also with you.

The ministers and the assembly may greet one another with a gesture of Christ's peace, and may say these or similar words: Peace be with you.

MEAL

GATHERING OF GIFTS

Gifts may be gathered for those in need and for the mission of the church.

SETTING THE TABLE

The table of the eucharistic meal is prepared. "Let the vineyards be fruitful" (R332–R333), "Create in me a clean heart" (R334), or another appropriate canticle, song, or hymn may be sung as bread, wine, money, and other gifts are brought to the table. A brief prayer may follow.

GREAT THANKSGIVING

The presiding minister greets the assembly and invites all present to give thanks:

The Lord be with you. **And al - so with you.**

Lift up your hearts. **We lift them to the Lord.**

Let us give thanks to the Lord our God.

It is right to give our thanks and praise.

The presiding minister continues with an initial thanksgiving:

It is indeed right, our duty and our joy . . .
(Here the minister may use the initial thanksgiving appointed for the day or season, concluding:)
. . . join their unending hymn:

R308   R335, R338 ▸

Ho - ly, ho - ly, ho - ly Lord, God of pow-er and
might, heav-en and earth are full of your
glo - ry. Ho - san - na in the high - est.
Bless-ed is he who comes in the name of the
Lord. Ho - san - na in the high - est,
ho - san - na in the high - est.

The presiding minister continues the thanksgiving, using one of the following forms.

A   *The presiding minister leads a prayer of thanksgiving at table. The following acclamation may be sung as part of the prayer:*

At the conclusion of the prayer:

The Lord's Prayer concludes the great thanksgiving:

Gathered into one by the Holy Spirit, let us pray as Jesus taught us:

A

Our Father in heaven,
   hallowed be your name,
   your kingdom come,
   your will be done,
     on earth as in heaven.
Give us today our daily bread.
Forgive us our sins
   as we forgive those
     who sin against us.
Save us from the time of trial
   and deliver us from evil.
For the kingdom, the power,
   and the glory are yours,
   now and forever. Amen.

B

Our Father, who art in heaven,
   hallowed be thy name,
   thy kingdom come,
   thy will be done,
     on earth as it is in heaven.
Give us this day our daily bread;
and forgive us our trespasses,
   as we forgive those
     who trespass against us;
and lead us not into temptation,
   but deliver us from evil.
For thine is the kingdom,
   and the power, and the glory,
   forever and ever. Amen.

The presiding minister proclaims the promise of Jesus' gift through this meal, using the words of institution.

The Lord's Prayer concludes the great thanksgiving. This form or one of those on page 34 may be used.

Gathered into one by the Ho - ly Spir - it, let us pray as Je - sus taught us:

Our Fa - ther in heav - en, hal - lowed be your name,

your king - dom come, your will be done, on earth as in

heav - en. Give us to - day our dai - ly bread.

For - give us our sins as we for - give those who sin a - gainst us.

Save us from the time of tri - al and de - liv - er us from e - vil.

For the king - dom, the pow'r, and the glo - ry are yours,

now and for - ev - er. A - men.

COMMUNION

The presiding minister may raise the bread and cup and address the assembly with these or similar words:

A

Holy things for holy people.
One is holy, one is Lord,
Jesus Christ, to the glory of God.

B

The gifts of God for the people of God.
Thanks be to God.

The assisting minister may conclude the invitation to the meal:
Taste and see that the Lord is good.

The bread may be broken for the communion.

When giving the bread and cup, the communion ministers say:
The body of Christ, given for you. The blood of Christ, shed for you.
and the communicant may respond, Amen.

The ministers commune either after or before the communion of the assembly.

Communion Song
Assembly song and other music may accompany the breaking of bread and the communion of the people, and may begin with "Lamb of God."   R341–R343 ▶

At the conclusion of the communion, "Now, Lord, you let your servant go" or another appropriate song may be sung as the table is cleared.   R344–R346 ▶

Communion Prayer
An assisting minister leads one of these or a similar prayer:
Let us pray.

A

We give you thanks, almighty God,
that you have refreshed us
through the healing power
of this gift of life.
In your mercy
strengthen us through this gift
in faith toward you
and in fervent love toward one another;
for the sake of Jesus Christ our Lord.
Amen.

B

O God, we give you thanks
that you have set before us this feast,
the body and blood of your Son.
By your Spirit
strengthen us to serve all in want
and to give ourselves away
as bread for the hungry,
through Jesus Christ our Lord.
Amen.

SENDING

SENDING OF COMMUNION MINISTERS

Communion ministers may be sent to bring the sacrament to those who are absent. The presiding minister may lead a prayer of sending.

Brief announcements related to the assembly's mission in the world may be made.

BLESSING

The presiding minister blesses the assembly with one of these or another appropriate blessing:

A	B	C
Holy Eternal Majesty,	The Lord bless you	Almighty God,
Holy Incarnate Word,	and keep you.	Father, ✝ Son,
Holy Abiding Spirit,	The Lord's face shine on you	and Holy Spirit,
one God, ✝ bless you	with grace and mercy.	bless you
now and forever.	The Lord look upon you	now and forever.
Amen.	with favor	**Amen.**
	and ✝ give you peace.	
	Amen.	

SENDING SONG

If "Now, Lord, you let your servant go" was not sung at the end of the communion, it may be sung here, or another sending song may be sung. The ministers may move to the door.

SENDING

The assisting minister sends the assembly forth with these or similar words:

A	B	C
Go in peace.	Go in peace.	Go in peace.
Share the good news.	Remember the poor.	Serve the Lord.
Thanks be to God.	**Thanks be to God.**	**Thanks be to God.**

WORD and THANKSGIVING
Shape of the Rite

GATHERING

The Holy Spirit gathers us in unity.

WORD

God speaks to us in scriptures read, sung, and preached.

THANKSGIVING

God's grace and mercy summons us to give thanks.

Hymn or Prayer — *We begin our thanksgiving with words sung or spoken.*

Gathering of Gifts — *We gather gifts for those in need and the church's mission.*

Thanksgiving for the Word — *We remember God's deeds of love and give thanks for them.*

Lord's Prayer — *Empowered by the Spirit, we are bold to pray the prayer Jesus taught.*

SENDING

God blesses us and sends us in mission to the world.

Blessing — *God blesses us and sends us in mission to the world.*

Sending Song — *Singing, we go out from the assembly as God's people in mission.*

Sending — *We bless the Lord and give thanks in word and deed.*

Central elements of the liturgy are noted in bold letters; other elements support and reveal the essential shape of Christian worship.

✠ WORD and THANKSGIVING

Word and Thanksgiving is a pattern for worship on those occasions when the liturgy does not include the Lord's supper.

GATHERING and WORD

The liturgy of Word and Thanksgiving begins with the gathering and word sections from Holy Communion. The liturgy then concludes with the thanksgiving and sending sections that follow here.

THANKSGIVING

GATHERING OF GIFTS

Gifts may be gathered for those in need and for the mission of the church. A hymn of praise and thanksgiving may be sung during or after the gathering of gifts.

THANKSGIVING FOR THE WORD

The following or a similar prayer of thanksgiving is said or sung:
The Lord be with you.
And also with you.

Let us give thanks to the Lord our God.
It is right to give our thanks and praise.

Praise and thanks to you, holy God,
for by your Word you made all things:
you spoke light into darkness,
called forth beauty from chaos,
and brought life into being.
Praise and thanks to you, holy God,
for your Word of life.

By your Word you called a people
to tell of your wonderful deeds:
freedom from captivity,
water on the desert journey,
a pathway home from exile.
Praise and thanks to you, holy God,
for your Word of life.

Mindful of your covenant,
you spoke of old by the prophets:
words of warning and of woe,
words to challenge and console,
wisdom for our life with you.
Praise and thanks to you, holy God,
for your Word of life.

Now you call to us through Jesus,
your Word made flesh among us:
light for those who dwell in darkness,
life to those entombed by death,
the way of your self-giving love.
Praise and thanks to you, holy God,
for your Word of life.

Send your Spirit of truth, O God;
rekindle your gifts within us:
renew our faith,
increase our hope,
and deepen our love
for the sake of a world in need.

Be faithful to your word, O God;
draw near to those who call on you:
lift up the weak and lowly;
bring justice to the hungry;
guide us in the ways of peace,
for you alone are God,
to you alone we sing our praise.

The assembly sings this canticle of praise or another appropriate song:

R311

Sal - va - tion be - longs to our God and to Christ the Lamb for -
ev - er and ev - er. Great and won - der - ful are your deeds, O

God of the u-ni-verse; just and true are your ways, O Rul-er of all the na-tions. Who can fail to hon-or you, Lord, and sing the glo-ry of your name? Sal - va-tion be-longs to our God and to Christ the Lamb for - ev - er and ev - er. For you a - lone are the Ho - ly One, and bless-ed is the one whose name is the Word of God. All praise and thanks to you, ho - ly God! Sal - va-tion be-longs to our God and to Christ the Lamb for - ev - er and ev - er.

Gathered into one by the Holy Spirit, let us pray as Jesus taught us:

A

Our Father in heaven,
   hallowed be your name,
   your kingdom come,
   your will be done,
     on earth as in heaven.
Give us today our daily bread.
Forgive us our sins
   as we forgive those
     who sin against us.
Save us from the time of trial
   and deliver us from evil.
For the kingdom, the power,
   and the glory are yours,
   now and forever. Amen.

B

Our Father, who art in heaven,
   hallowed be thy name,
   thy kingdom come,
   thy will be done,
     on earth as it is in heaven.
Give us this day our daily bread;
and forgive us our trespasses,
   as we forgive those
     who trespass against us;
and lead us not into temptation,
   but deliver us from evil.
For thine is the kingdom,
   and the power, and the glory,
   forever and ever. Amen.

SENDING

Brief announcements related to the assembly's mission in the world may be made.

BLESSING

The presiding minister blesses the assembly:
Go forth into the world to serve God with gladness;
be of good courage;
hold fast to that which is good;
render to no one evil for evil;
strengthen the fainthearted;
support the weak;
help the afflicted;
honor all people;
love and serve God,
rejoicing in the power of the Holy Spirit.

A

Almighty God,
Father, ☩ Son,
and Holy Spirit,
bless you now and forever.
Amen.

B

The Lord bless you and keep you.
The Lord's face shine on you
with grace and mercy.
The Lord look upon you with favor
and ☩ give you peace.
Amen.

SENDING SONG

A sending hymn or song may be sung.

SENDING

The assisting minister may send the assembly forth:
Let us bless the Lord.
Thanks be to God.

HOLY BAPTISM
Shape of the Rite

The context for the liturgy of baptism is ordinarily the primary Sunday assembly of the congregation around word and table. As an alternative to the following Shape of the Rite, the liturgy of baptism may also replace the remembrance of baptism in the gathering rite.

GATHERING

WORD
Readings and Responses
Sermon
Hymn of the Day

BAPTISM
Presentation
   Introduction
   Presentation
Profession
   Renunciation of Evil
   Profession of Faith
Baptism
   Thanksgiving
   Baptism
   Laying On of Hands
   Signing with the Cross
   Clothing with a Garment
Welcome
   Presentation of a Candle
   Welcome
Prayers of Intercession
Peace

MEAL

SENDING

Central elements of the liturgy are noted in bold letters; other elements support and reveal the essential shape of Christian worship.

 # HOLY BAPTISM

PRESENTATION

Candidates for baptism, sponsors, and parents gather with the ministers at the font.

INTRODUCTION

The presiding minister may address the assembly in these or similar words:
God, who is rich in mercy and love, gives us a new birth into a living hope through the sacrament of baptism. The power of sin is put to death in this holy flood, and we are raised with Jesus Christ to new life. We are united with all the baptized in the one body of Christ, anointed with the gift of the Holy Spirit, and sent out in mission for the life of the world.

PRESENTATION

One or more sponsors for each candidate, in turn, present the candidates:
I present *name* for baptism.

The presiding minister addresses candidates who are able to answer for themselves:
Name, trusting in the grace and love of God, do you desire to be baptized?
Each candidate responds: I do.

The presiding minister addresses parents of children who are not able to answer for themselves:
Trusting in the grace and love of God, do you desire to have your *children* baptized?
Response: I do.

The presiding minister may also address parents in these or similar words:
As you present your *children* for baptism,
you are entrusted with gifts and responsibilities:
to live with *them* among God's faithful people,
bring *them* to the word of God and the holy supper,
and nurture *them* in faith and prayer,
so that *they* may learn to trust God,
proclaim Christ through word and deed,
care for others and the world God made,
and work for justice and peace among all people.
Name/s, do you promise to help your *children* grow
in the Christian faith and life?
Response: I do.

The presiding minister addresses sponsors in these or similar words:
Sponsors, do you promise to nurture *these persons*
in the Christian faith as you are empowered by God's Spirit,
and to help *them* live in the covenant of baptism
and in communion with the church?
Response: I do.

The presiding minister addresses the assembly:
People of God, do you promise to support *name/s*
and pray for *them* in *their* new life in Christ?
We do.

PROFESSION

RENUNCIATION OF EVIL

The presiding minister addresses candidates and the parents and sponsors of young children:

A	B
I ask you to reject sin, profess your faith in Christ, and confess the faith of the church.	I ask you to reject sin, profess your faith in Christ, and confess the faith of the church.

A
I ask you to reject sin,
profess your faith in Christ,
and confess the faith of the church.

Do you renounce the devil
   and all the forces that defy God,
the powers of this world
   that rebel against God,
and the ways of sin
   that draw you from God?
Response: I do.

B
I ask you to reject sin,
profess your faith in Christ,
and confess the faith of the church.

Do you renounce the devil
   and all the forces that defy God?
Response: I renounce them.

Do you renounce the powers of this world
   that rebel against God?
Response: I renounce them.

Do you renounce the ways of sin
   that draw you from God?
Response: I renounce them.

PROFESSION OF FAITH

The presiding minister may also ask the candidates and the parents and sponsors of young children:

A
Do you turn to Christ
   as your Lord and Savior?
Response: I do.

B
Do you turn to Christ
   as your Lord and Savior?
Response: In faith I turn to Christ.

With the whole church, let us confess our faith.

Do you believe in God the Father?
I believe in God, the Father almighty,
creator of heaven and earth.

Do you believe in Jesus Christ, the Son of God?
I believe in Jesus Christ, God's only Son, our Lord,
who was conceived by the Holy Spirit,
born of the virgin Mary,
suffered under Pontius Pilate,
was crucified, died, and was buried;
he descended to the dead.
On the third day he rose again;
he ascended into heaven,
he is seated at the right hand of the Father,
and he will come to judge the living and the dead.

Do you believe in God the Holy Spirit?
I believe in the Holy Spirit,
the holy catholic church,
the communion of saints,
the forgiveness of sins,
the resurrection of the body,
and the life everlasting. Amen.

BAPTISM

THANKSGIVING

Water may be poured into the font before or during the thanksgiving.

Standing at the font, the presiding minister begins the thanksgiving:
The Lord be with you.
And also with you.

Let us give thanks to the Lord our God.
It is right to give our thanks and praise.

The presiding minister continues the thanksgiving with this or another prayer of thanksgiving:
We give you thanks, O God,
for in the beginning your Spirit brooded over the waters
and you created the world by your Word,
calling forth life in which you took delight.

Through water you led your people Israel
from slavery in Egypt to freedom in the promised land.
In the waters of the Jordan
Jesus was baptized by John and anointed with the Holy Spirit.
By the baptism of Jesus' death and resurrection
you delivered us from the power of sin and death
and set us free to live in you.

Send your Holy Spirit upon this water
and upon *all* who *are* washed in it,
that *they* may be given new life.
To you be given honor and praise
through Jesus Christ our Lord,
in the unity of the Holy Spirit, now and forever.
Amen.

BAPTISM

The candidate is immersed into the water, or water is poured on the candidate's head, as the presiding minister says:
Name, I baptize you in the name of the Father,
The candidate is immersed, or water is poured on the candidate's head a second time:
and of the Son,
The candidate is immersed, or water is poured on the candidate's head a third time:
and of the Holy Spirit.
Amen.

The assembly may also respond with one of the following or another appropriate acclamation:

A	B	R349–R355 ▸
You belong to Christ,	**Blessed be God,**	
in whom you have been baptized.	**the source of all life,**	
Alleluia.	**the word of salvation,**	
Alleluia.	**the spirit of mercy.**	

LAYING ON OF HANDS

The presiding minister continues:
Let us pray.
We give you thanks, O God,
that through water and the Holy Spirit
you give your daughters and sons new birth,
wash them from sin, and raise them to eternal life.
The presiding minister lays both hands on the head of each newly baptized person and prays for each:
Sustain *name* with the gift of your Holy Spirit:
the spirit of wisdom and understanding,
the spirit of counsel and might,
the spirit of knowledge and the fear of the Lord,
the spirit of joy in your presence,
both now and forever.
Amen.

SIGNING WITH THE CROSS

The presiding minister marks the sign of the cross on the forehead of each of the baptized.
Oil prepared for this purpose may be used. As the sign of the cross is made, the minister says:
Name, child of God,
you have been sealed by the Holy Spirit
and marked with the cross of Christ forever.
Amen.

CLOTHING WITH A GARMENT

The newly baptized may receive a baptismal garment. The following words may also be said:
You have been clothed in Christ.
All who are baptized into Christ have put on Christ.

WELCOME

PRESENTATION OF A CANDLE

A lighted candle may be given to each of the newly baptized (to a sponsor of a young child) as a representative of the congregation says:
Walk in the faith of Christ crucified and risen.
Shine with the light of Christ.

WELCOME

The ministers and the baptismal group face the assembly. A representative of the congregation welcomes the newly baptized in these or similar words:
Through baptism you have been received into the household of God,
entrusted with the good news of Jesus Christ,
and strengthened to serve by the holy and life-giving Spirit.

The assembly may also offer a welcome in these or similar words:
We welcome you into the body of Christ
and the mission we share.
Join us as we give praise to God
and bear God's creative and redeeming word to all the world.

Those who have gathered at the font may return to their places. A psalm or hymn may be sung.

SERVICE MUSIC
Contents

Gathering Song
Kyrie   R312–R317
Holy God   R318–R319
Glory to God   R320–R322
This Is the Feast   R323–R324

Gospel Acclamations
Alleluia   R325–R329
Lenten Acclamation   R330

Response to Intercessions   R331

Setting the Table
Let the Vineyards Be Fruitful   R332–R333
Create in Me   R334

Acclamations at Table   R335–R340

Communion Song
Lamb of God   R341–R343
Now, Lord, You Let Your Servant Go   R344–R346

Baptism, Remembrance of Baptism   R347–R355

Marriage   R356–R357

Healing   R358–R362

Funeral   R363–R366

Kyrie
Litany

Leader

In peace, let us pray to the Lord.

Assembly

Lord, have mer - cy.

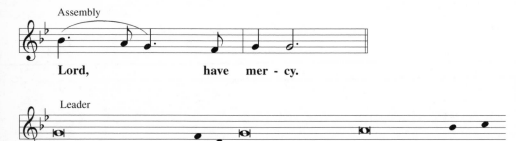

Leader

For the peace from a-bove, and for our sal-vation, let us pray to the Lord.

Assembly

Lord, have mer - cy.

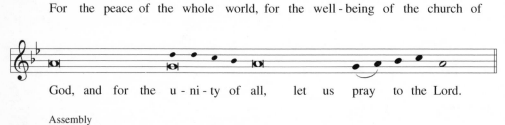

Leader

For the peace of the whole world, for the well-being of the church of

God, and for the u - ni - ty of all, let us pray to the Lord.

Assembly

Lord, have mer - cy.

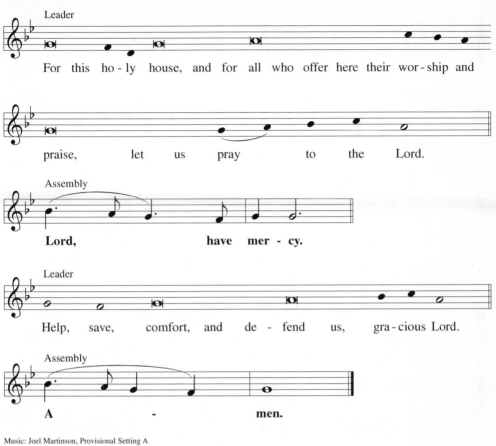

Leader
For this ho-ly house, and for all who offer here their wor-ship and praise, let us pray to the Lord.

Assembly
Lord, have mer - cy.

Leader
Help, save, comfort, and de - fend us, gra - cious Lord.

Assembly
A - men.

Music: Joel Martinson, Provisional Setting A
Music © 2004 Augsburg Fortress

R 313

Kyrie
Litany

Leader: In peace, let us pray to the Lord. **Lord, have mer-cy.**

Leader: For the peace from a-bove, and for our sal-va-tion, let us pray to the Lord. **Lord, have mer-cy.**

Leader: For the peace of the whole world, for the well-be-ing of the church of God, and for the u-ni-ty of all, let us pray to the Lord. **Lord, have mer-cy.**

Leader: For this ho-ly house, and for all who of-fer here their wor-ship and praise, let us pray to the Lord. **Lord, have mer-cy.**

Leader: Help, save, com-fort, and de-fend us, gra-cious Lord. **A - men.**

Music: Marty Haugen, Provisional Setting B
Music © 2004 Augsburg Fortress

Kyrie
Ninefold

Lord, have mer - cy, Lord, have mer - cy,

Lord, have mer - cy.

Christ, have mer - cy, Christ, have mer - cy,

Christ, have mer - cy.

Lord, have mer - cy, Lord, have mer - cy,

Lord, have mer - cy.

Music: Joel Martinson, Provisional Setting A
Music © 2004 Augsburg Fortress

R315

Kyrie
Nkosi, Nkosi

Lord, have mer - cy; have mer - cy up - on us.
Nko - si, Nko - si, yi - ba nen - ce - ba.

Christ, have mer - cy; have mer - cy up - on us.
Kres - tu, Kres - tu, yi - ba nen - ce - ba.

Lord, have mer - cy; have mer - cy up - on us.
Nko - si, Nko - si, yi - ba nen - ce - ba.

Kyrie
Lord, have mercy

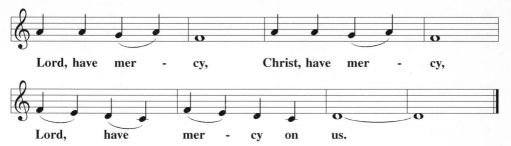

Lord, have mer - cy, Christ, have mer - cy,

Lord, have mer - cy on us.

Music: Swee Hong Lim
Music © General Board of Global Ministries, GBGMusik. Used by permission.
You must contact GBGMusik at 475 Riverside Dr., Room 350, New York, NY 10115 for permission to reproduce this selection.

Kyrie
Sixfold

R 317

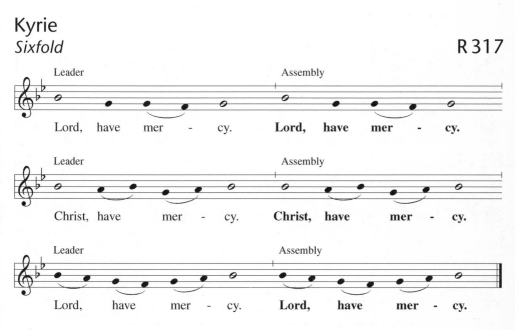

Leader — Assembly

Lord, have mer - cy. **Lord, have mer - cy.**

Leader — Assembly

Christ, have mer - cy. **Christ, have mer - cy.**

Leader — Assembly

Lord, have mer - cy. **Lord, have mer - cy.**

Music: Traditional plainsong

R 318

Holy God
Trisagion

Ho - ly, ho - ly, ho - ly God, ho - ly and might - y, ho - ly and im - mor - tal, have mer - cy on us.

Music: Traditional Russian Orthodox

Holy God
Trisagion

R 319

Ho - ly God, ho - ly and might - y, ho - ly and im-mor - tal, have mer - cy on us.

Music: Mark Mummert
Music © 2003 Augsburg Fortress

Glory to God

R 320

Glo-ry to God in the high - est, and peace to God's peo-ple on earth.

Glo-ry to God in the high - est, and peace to God's peo-ple on earth.

Lord God, heav'n-ly King, al - might-y God and Fa-ther, we

wor-ship you, we give you thanks, we praise you for your glo - ry.

Glo-ry to God in the high - est, and peace to God's peo-ple on earth.

Lord Je - sus Christ, on-ly Son of the Fa - ther, Lord

God, Lamb of God, you take a - way the sin of the

world: have mer - cy on us; you are seat - ed at the

right hand of the Fa - ther: re - ceive our prayer.

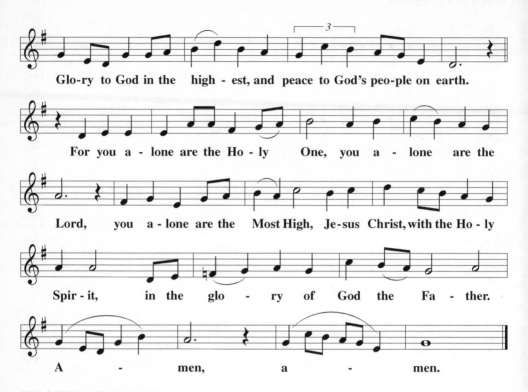

Glo-ry to God in the high - est, and peace to God's peo-ple on earth.

For you a - lone are the Ho - ly One, you a - lone are the

Lord, you a - lone are the Most High, Je-sus Christ, with the Ho - ly

Spir - it, in the glo - ry of God the Fa - ther.

A - men, a - men.

Music: Joel Martinson, Provisional Setting A
Music © 2004 Augsburg Fortress

Glory to God

Glo-ry to God in the high-est, and peace to God's peo-ple on earth.

Glo-ry to God in the high-est, and peace to God's peo-ple on earth.

Lord God, heav-en-ly King, al-might-y God and Fa-ther, we

wor-ship you, we give you thanks, we praise you for your glo-ry.

Glo-ry to God in the high-est, and peace to God's peo-ple on earth.

Glo-ry to God in the high-est, and peace to God's peo-ple on earth.

Lord Je-sus Christ, on-ly Son of the Fa-ther,

Lord God, Lamb of God, you take a-way the sin of the world: have

mer-cy on us; you are seat-ed at the

right hand of the Fa-ther: re-ceive our prayer.

Glo-ry to God in the high-est, and peace to God's peo-ple on earth.

Glo-ry to God in the high-est, and peace to God's peo-ple on earth.

For you a-lone are the Ho-ly One, you a-lone are the Lord,

you a-lone are the Most High, Je-sus Christ, with the

Ho-ly Spir-it, in the glo-ry of God the Fa-ther. A-men.

Glo-ry to God in the high-est, and peace to God's peo-ple on earth.

Glo-ry to God in the high-est, and peace to God's peo-ple on earth.

Music: Marty Haugen, Provisional Setting B
Music © 2004 Augsburg Fortress

Glory to God

Glo-ry to God in the high-est, and peace to God's peo-ple on earth.

Lord God, heav-en-ly King, al-might-y God and Fa-ther,

we wor-ship you, we give you thanks, we praise you for your glo-ry.

Lord Je-sus Christ, on-ly Son of the Fa-ther,

Lord God, Lamb of God, you take a-way the sin of the world:

have mer-cy on us; you are seat-ed at the right hand of the Fa-ther:

re-ceive our prayer. For you a-lone are the Ho-ly One,

you a-lone are the Lord, you a-lone are the Most High,

Je-sus Christ, with the Ho-ly Spir-it,

in the glo-ry of God the Fa-ther. A - men.

Music: David Hurd

R 323

This Is the Feast

This is the feast of vic - to - ry for our God.

Al - le - lu - ia, al - le - lu - ia.

Wor - thy is Christ, the Lamb who was slain, whose

blood set us free to be peo - ple of God.

Pow - er, rich - es, wis - dom and strength, and

hon - or, bless - ing and glo - ry are his.

This is the feast of vic - to - ry for our God.

Al - le - lu - ia, al - le - lu - ia.

Sing with all the peo - ple of God, and

join in the hymn of all cre - a - tion:

Bless - ing, hon - or, glo - ry and might be to

God and the Lamb for - ev - er. A - men.

This is the feast of vic - to - ry for our God,

for the Lamb who was slain has be - gun his reign.

Al - le - lu - ia, al - le - lu - ia, al - le - lu - ia.

Text: John W. Arthur, based on Rev. 5, 19
Music: Joel Martinson, Provisional Setting A
Text © 1978 *Lutheran Book of Worship,* admin. Augsburg Fortress
Music © 2004 Augsburg Fortress

R 324

This Is the Feast

This is the feast of vic - to - ry for our God. Al - le - lu - ia, al - le - lu - ia, al - le - lu - ia.

Wor - thy is Christ, the Lamb who was slain, whose blood set us free to be peo - ple of God.

Pow-er, rich - es, wis - dom and strength, and hon - or, bless - ing, and glo - ry are his.

This is the feast of vic - to - ry for our God. Al - le - lu - ia, al - le -

lu - ia, al - le - lu - ia.

Sing with all the peo - ple of God, and

join in the hymn of all cre - a - tion:

Bless - ing, hon - or, glo - ry and might be to

God and the Lamb for - ev - er. A - men.

This is the feast of vic - to - ry for our God,

for the Lamb who was slain has be - gun

his reign. Al - le - lu - ia,

al - le - lu - ia, al - le - lu - ia.

Text: John W. Arthur, based on Rev. 5, 19
Music: Marty Haugen, Provisional Setting B
Text © 1978 *Lutheran Book of Worship*, admin. Augsburg Fortress
Music © 2004 Augsburg Fortress

Alleluia
Verse of the Day

R 325

Al - le - lu - ia, al - le - lu - ia.

Al - le - lu - ia, al - le - lu - ia.

Fine

Verse (cantor or choir)

D.C. al Fine

Music: Joel Martinson, Provisional Setting A
Music © 2004 Augsburg Fortress

Alleluia
Lord, to whom shall we go?

R 326

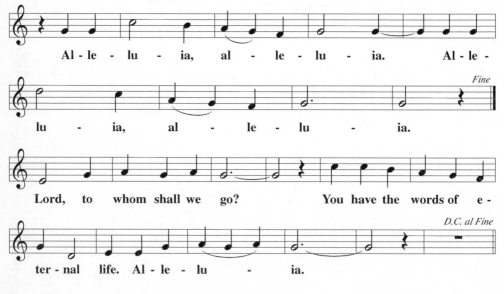

Al - le - lu - ia, al - le - lu - ia. Al - le -

lu - ia, al - le - lu - ia.

Fine

Lord, to whom shall we go? You have the words of e -

ter - nal life. Al - le - lu - ia.

D.C. al Fine

Music: Joel Martinson, Provisional Setting A
Music © 2004 Augsburg Fortress

Alleluia
Verse of the Day

Al - le - lu - ia, al - le - lu - ia.

Al - le - lu - ia.

Verse (cantor or choir)

Al - le - lu - ia, al - le - lu - ia.

Music: Marty Haugen, Provisional Setting B
Music © 2004 Augsburg Fortress

Alleluia
Your words are sweet

R 328

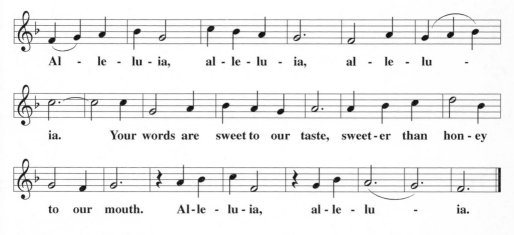

Al - le - lu - ia, al - le - lu - ia, al - le - lu -

ia. Your words are sweet to our taste, sweet-er than hon - ey

to our mouth. Al - le - lu - ia, al - le - lu - ia.

Music: Marty Haugen, Provisional Setting B
Music © 2004 Augsburg Fortress

R 329   Alleluia

Al - le - lu - ia, al - le - lu - ia, al - le - lu - ia.

Fine

Al - le - lu - ia, al - le - lu - ia, al - le - lu - ia.

Verse (cantor or choir)   *   *D.C. al Fine*

Al - le - lu - ia!

* Choose either part.

Music: Alleluia 7, Jacques Berthier and the Taizé Community
Music © 1984 Les Presses de Taizé, admin. GIA Publications, Inc. Used by permission.
You must contact GIA Publications at 800/GIA-1358 for permission to reproduce this selection.

R 330   Lenten Acclamation

Fine

Glo - ry to you, O   Word of God,   Lord   Je - sus   Christ.

Verse (cantor or choir)   *D.C. al Fine*

Music: Richard Proulx
Music © 1975 GIA Publications, Inc. All rights reserved. Used by permission.
You must contact GIA Publications at 800/GIA-1358 for permission to reproduce this selection.

Response to Intercessions
O Lord, hear our prayer

R 331

O Lord, hear our prayer we of-fer up to   you; O   Lord, hear our prayer.

Text and music: Ralph C. Sappington
Text and music © 1999 Augsburg Fortress

Let the Vineyards Be Fruitful

R 332

Let the vine-yards be fruit-ful, Lord, and

fill to the brim our cup of bless - ing.

Gath-er a har - vest from the seeds that were sown, that

we may be fed with the bread of life.

Gath - er the hopes and dreams of all; u -

nite them with the prayers we of - fer.

Grace our ta - ble with your pres - ence, and

give us a fore - taste of the feast to come.

Text: John W. Arthur
Music: Joel Martinson, Provisional Setting A
Text © 1978 *Lutheran Book of Worship*, admin. Augsburg Fortress
Music © 2004 Augsburg Fortress

R 333

Let the Vineyards Be Fruitful

Let the vine - yards be fruit - ful, Lord, and

fill to the brim our cup of bless - ing.

Gath - er a har - vest from the seeds that were sown, that

we may be fed with the bread of life.

Gath - er the hopes and the dreams of all, u -

nite them with the prayers we of - fer.

Grace our ta - ble with your pres - ence, and

give us a fore - taste of the feast to come.

Text: John W. Arthur
Music: Marty Haugen, Provisional Setting B
Text © 1978 *Lutheran Book of Worship,* admin. Augsburg Fortress
Music © 2004 Augsburg Fortress

Create in Me a Clean Heart

R 334

Cre - ate in me a clean heart, O God, and re -
new a right spir - it with - in me.
Cast me not a - way from your pres - ence, and take not your
Ho - ly Spir - it from me. Re -
store to me the joy of your sal - va - tion, and up -
hold me with your free Spir - it.
Cre - ate in me a clean heart, O God, and re -
new a right spir - it with - in me.

Music: James Capers, *Liturgy of Joy*; arr. Dennis Friesen-Carper, from *This Far by Faith*
Music © 1993, 1999 Augsburg Fortress

R 335

Holy, Holy, Holy

Ho - ly, ho - ly, ho - ly Lord, God of pow-er and might,

heav-en and earth are full of your glo-ry. Ho-san-na in the

high - est. Bless - ed is he who comes in the

name of the Lord. Ho - san - na in the

high - est, ho - san - na in the high - est.

Music: Per Harling
Music © 2004 Augsburg Fortress

Acclamation

R 336

Christ has died. Christ is ris - en. Christ will come a - gain.

Music: Per Harling
Music © 2004 Augsburg Fortress

Amen

R 337

A - men, a - men, a - men.

Music: Per Harling
Music © 2004 Augsburg Fortress

R 338 Holy, Holy, Holy

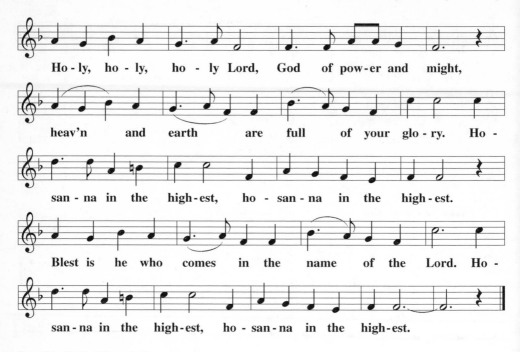

Ho - ly, ho - ly, ho - ly Lord, God of pow-er and might,

heav'n and earth are full of your glo - ry. Ho -

san - na in the high-est, ho - san - na in the high-est.

Blest is he who comes in the name of the Lord. Ho -

san - na in the high-est, ho - san - na in the high-est.

Music: Richard Proulx, *A Community Mass*
Music © 1971, 1977 GIA Publications, Inc. All rights reserved. Used by permission.
You must contact GIA Publications at 800/GIA-1358 for permission to reproduce this selection.

R 339 Acclamation

Christ has died. Christ is ris - en. Christ will come a - gain.

Music: Richard Proulx, *A Community Mass*
Music © 1971, 1977 GIA Publications, Inc. All rights reserved. Used by permission.
You must contact GIA Publications at 800/GIA-1358 for permission to reproduce this selection.

R 340 Amen

A - men, a - men, a - men.

Music: Richard Proulx, *A Community Mass*
Music © 1971, 1977 GIA Publications, Inc. All rights reserved. Used by permission.
You must contact GIA Publications at 800/GIA-1358 for permission to reproduce this selection.

Lamb of God

Lamb of God, you take a - way the sin of the world; have mer - cy on us. Lamb of God, you take a - way the sin of the world; have mer - cy on us. Lamb of God, you take a - way the sin of the world; grant us peace, grant us peace.

Music: Joel Martinson, Provisional Setting A
Music © 2004 Augsburg Fortress

R 342

Lamb of God

Lamb of God, you take a-way the sin of the world; have mer - cy on us.

Lamb of God, you take a-way the sin of the world; have mer - cy on us.

Lamb of God, you take a-way the sin of the world; grant us peace.

Music: Marty Haugen, Provisional Setting B
Music © 2004 Augsburg Fortress

Lamb of God
Cordero de Dios

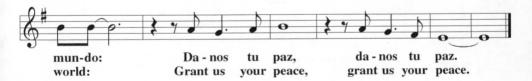

Spanish: Cor - de - ro de Dios, tú que qui - tas el pe - ca - do del
English: O Lamb of . . God, you . . take a - way the sin of the

mun-do: ten pie-dad de no - so - tros, ten pie-dad de no-
world: have mer-cy up - on us, have mer-cy up-

so-tros. Cor-de - ro de Dios, tú que qui-tas el pe-ca-do del
on us. O Lamb of . . God, you . . take a - way the sin of the

mun-do: ten pie-dad de no - so - tros, ten pie-dad de no-
world: have mer-cy up - on us, have mer-cy up-

so - tros. Cor-de - ro de Dios, tú que qui-tas el pe-ca-do del
on us. O Lamb of . . God, you . . take a - way the sin of the

mun-do: Da - nos tu paz, da - nos tu paz.
world: Grant us your peace, grant us your peace.

Music: Victor Jortack, from *Libro de Liturgia y Cántico*
Music © 1998 Augsburg Fortress

R 344

Now, Lord, You Let Your Servant Go

Now, Lord, you let your ser - vant go in peace: your
word has been ful - filled. My own eyes have
seen the sal - va - tion which you have pre - pared in the
sight of ev - 'ry peo - ple: a light to re - veal you to the
na - tions and the glo - ry of your peo - ple
Is - ra - el. Glo - ry to the Fa - ther, and
to the Son, and to the Ho - ly Spir - it,
as it was in the be - gin - ning, is
now, and will be for - ev - er. A -
men, a - men, a - men.

Music: Joel Martinson, Provisional Setting A
Music © 2004 Augsburg Fortress

Now, Lord, You Let Your Servant Go

R 345

Now, Lord, you let your ser-vant go in peace: your word has been ful-filled. My own eyes have seen the sal-va-tion which you have pre-pared in the sight of ev-'ry peo-ple: a light to re-veal you to the na-tions and the glo-ry of your peo-ple Is-ra-el. Glo-ry to the Fa-ther, and to the Son, and to the Ho-ly Spir-it: as it was in the be-gin-ning, is now, and will be for-ev-er. A-men.

Music: Marty Haugen, Provisional Setting B
Music © 2004 Augsburg Fortress

R 346

Now, Lord, You Let Your Servant Go

Now, Lord, you let your servant go in peace: your word has been ful-filled.

My own eyes have seen the sal-va-tion which you have prepared in the sight of

ev - 'ry peo - ple: a light to reveal you to the na - tions

and the glory of your peo - ple Is - ra - el.

Glo - ry to the Father, and to the Son, and to the Ho - ly Spir - it:

as it was in the beginning, is now, and will be for - ev - er. A - men.

Music: Traditional plainsong

You Belong to Christ

R 347

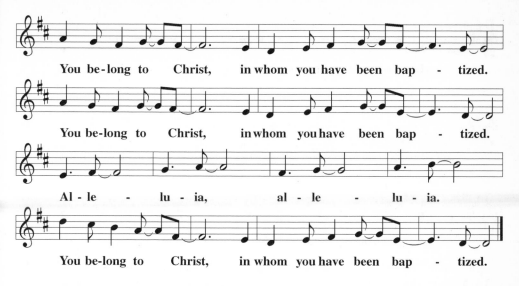

You be-long to Christ, in whom you have been bap - tized.

You be-long to Christ, in whom you have been bap - tized.

Al - le - lu - ia, al - le - lu - ia.

You be-long to Christ, in whom you have been bap - tized.

Text: Gal. 3:27, 29, adapt. *Holy Baptism and Related Rites,* Renewing Worship, vol. 3
Music: Ralph C. Sappington
Text © 2002 Augsburg Fortress
Music © 2003 Augsburg Fortress

You Belong to Christ

R 348

You be - long to Christ, in whom you have been bap - tized.

al - le - lu - ia.

Al - le - lu - ia, al - le - lu - ia, al - le - lu - ia.

Text: Gal. 3:27, 29, adapt. *Holy Baptism and Related Rites,* Renewing Worship, vol. 3
Music: Robert A. Hobby
Text © 2002 Augsburg Fortress
Music © 2004 Augsburg Fortress

R 349 Blessed Be God, the Source of All Life

Bless - ed be God, the source of all life, the word of sal - va - tion, the spir - it of mer - cy.

Text: *Holy Baptism and Related Rites,* Renewing Worship, vol. 3
Music: Carl Schalk
Text © 2002 Augsburg Fortress
Music © 2003 Augsburg Fortress

R 350 Blessed Be God, the Source of All Life

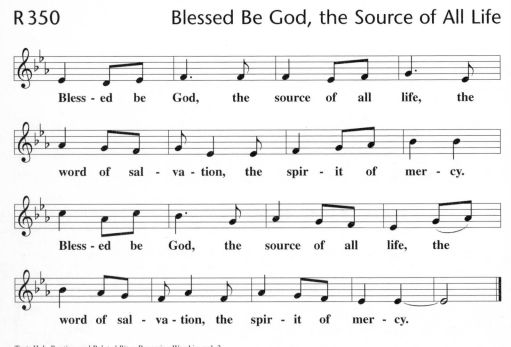

Bless - ed be God, the source of all life, the word of sal - va - tion, the spir - it of mer - cy. Bless - ed be God, the source of all life, the word of sal - va - tion, the spir - it of mer - cy.

Text: *Holy Baptism and Related Rites,* Renewing Worship, vol. 3
Music: Rawn Harbor
Text © 2002 Augsburg Fortress
Music © 2004 Augsburg Fortress

Praise to the Blessed and Holy Trinity R 351

Praise to the blessed and ho - ly Trin - i - ty, one God, who

gives us life, sal - va - tion, and re - sur - rec - tion.

Text: *Holy Baptism and Related Rites,* Renewing Worship, vol. 3
Music: Rawn Harbor
Text © 2002 Augsburg Fortress
Music © 2003 Augsburg Fortress

Praise to the Blessed and Holy Trinity R 352

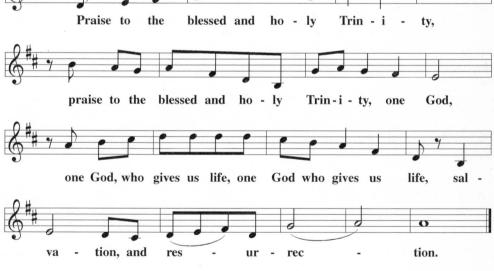

Praise to the blessed and ho - ly Trin - i - ty,

praise to the blessed and ho - ly Trin - i - ty, one God,

one God, who gives us life, one God who gives us life, sal -

va - tion, and res - ur - rec - tion.

Text: *Holy Baptism and Related Rites,* Renewing Worship, vol. 3
Music: Richard Hillert
Text © 2002 Augsburg Fortress
Music © 2004 Augsburg Fortress

R 353　　Blessed Be God, Who Chose You

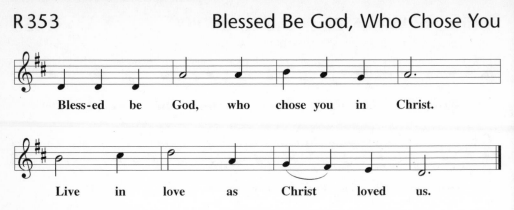

Text: *Welcome to Christ: Lutheran Rites for the Catechumenate; Holy Baptism and Related Rites,* Renewing Worship, vol. 3
Music: Anne Krentz Organ
Text © 1997 Augsburg Fortress
Music © 2003 Augsburg Fortress

R 354　　Blessed Be God, Who Chose You

Text: *Welcome to Christ: Lutheran Rites for the Catechumenate; Holy Baptism and Related Rites,* Renewing Worship, vol. 3
Music: José Ruiz
Text © 1997 Augsburg Fortress
Music © 2004 Augsburg Fortress

Springs of Water, Bless the Lord

R 355

Refrain

Springs of wa - ter, bless the Lord.

Give God glo - ry and praise for - ev - er.

Verses (cantor or choir:)

Buried with	Christ	in	death,	you are
Bathed in the	foun-tain	of	life,	you are
You are God's	work	of	art,	cre -
You be -	long	to	Christ,	in
All of	you	are	one,	u -
Re - joice, all	you	bap -	tized,	

to refrain

raised with	him	to	life.
born to a	liv -	ing	hope.
ated	in	Christ	Jesus.
whom you have	been	bap -	tized.
nited	in	Christ	Jesus.
called to be	chil - dren	of	God.

Text: *Welcome to Christ: Lutheran Rites for the Catechumenate*
Music: Robert Buckley Farlee
Text and music © 1997 Augsburg Fortress

R 356

God Is Love

God is love; let us love one an-oth-er as God first loved us.

Text: 1 John 4:12, 16, adapt. *Life Passages: Marriage, Healing, Funeral,* Renewing Worship, vol. 4
Music: Ben Houge
Text © 2002 Augsburg Fortress
Music © 2003 Augsburg Fortress

R 357

May the Blessing of God

May the bless-ing of God set a seal on your hearts to strength-en you in faith-ful-ness and love, to strength-en you in faith-ful-ness and love.

Text: *Life Passages: Marriage, Healing, Funeral,* Renewing Worship, vol. 4
Music: Jay Beech
Text © 2002 Augsburg Fortress
Music © 2003 Augsburg Fortress

Healer of Boundless Compassion

R 358

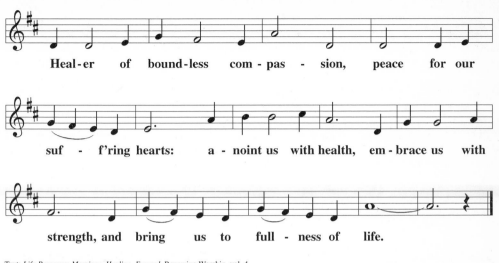

Heal-er of bound-less com-pas - sion, peace for our suf - f'ring hearts: a - noint us with health, em-brace us with strength, and bring us to full - ness of life.

Text: *Life Passages: Marriage, Healing, Funeral,* Renewing Worship, vol. 4
Music: Russell Schulz-Widmar
Text © 2002 Augsburg Fortress
Music © 2003 Augsburg Fortress

Healer of Boundless Compassion

R 359

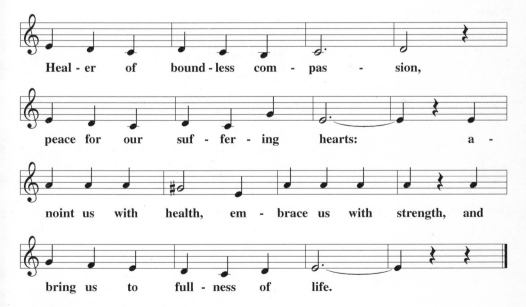

Heal - er of bound - less com - pas - sion, peace for our suf - fer - ing hearts: a - noint us with health, em - brace us with strength, and bring us to full - ness of life.

Text: *Life Passages: Marriage, Healing, Funeral,* Renewing Worship, vol. 4
Music: Jay Beech
Text © 2002 Augsburg Fortress
Music © 2004 Augsburg Fortress

R 360

You Anoint My Head

You a - noint my head with oil and my

cup is run - ning o - ver.

Text: *Life Passages: Marriage, Healing, Funeral*, Renewing Worship, vol. 4
Music: May Schwarz
Text © 2002 Augsburg Fortress
Music © 2004 Augsburg Fortress

R 361

Blessed Be God, Who Forgives

Bles-sed be God, who for - gives all our sins, who

heals all our ills, who crowns us with mer-cy and love.

Text: *Life Passages: Marriage, Healing, Funeral*, Renewing Worship, vol. 4
Music: Anne Krentz Organ
Text © 2002 Augsburg Fortress
Music © 2004 Augsburg Fortress

May the God of All Healing

R 362

May the God of all heal-ing en - fold us in love,
fill us with peace, and lead us to whole - ness and strength.

Text: *Life Passages: Marriage, Healing, Funeral*, Renewing Worship, vol. 4
Music: Jayne Southwick Cool
Text © 2002 Augsburg Fortress
Music © 2003 Augsburg Fortress

O God, You Have Been Our Refuge

R 363

Al - le - lu - ia, al - le - lu - ia.
O God, you have been our ref-uge from one gen-er-a-tion to an -
oth - er. Al - le - lu - ia, al - le - lu - ia.

Text: Ps. 90:1, *Book of Common Prayer; Life Passages: Marriage, Healing, Funeral*, Renewing Worship, vol. 4
Music: Carl Schalk
Music © 2003 Augsburg Fortress

R 364

Give Rest, O Christ

Give rest, O Christ, to your ser-vant with your saints, where sor -
row and pain are no more, nei-ther sigh - ing, but
life ev - er - last - ing.

Text: *Book of Common Prayer; Life Passages: Marriage, Healing, Funeral,* Renewing Worship, vol. 4
Music: José Ruiz
Music © 2003 Augsburg Fortress

R 365

All of Us Go Down to the Dust

All of us go down to the dust, yet e - ven at the grave we
make our song: Al - le - lu - ia, al - le - lu - ia,
al - le - lu - ia, al - le - lu - ia.

Text: Traditional; *Life Passages: Marriage, Healing, Funeral,* Renewing Worship, vol. 4
Music: Mark Mummert
Music © 2003 Augsburg Fortress

Into Paradise

R 366

Into paradise may the angels lead you. At your coming may the martyrs receive you, and lead you into the holy city, Jerusalem, Jerusalem. May a choir of angels welcome you, and where Lazarus is poor no more, may you have everlasting rest, may you have everlasting rest, may you have everlasting rest.

Text: Traditional, adapt. *Life Passages: Marriage, Healing, Funeral,* Renewing Worship, vol. 4
Music: Rawn Harbor
Text © 2002 Augsburg Fortress
Music © 2003 Augsburg Fortress

Acknowledgments

Renewing Worship Liturgies contains assembly versions of materials first prepared for *Holy Communion and Related Rites,* Renewing Worship, vol. 6 (Augsburg Fortress, 2004), as well as selections from *Holy Baptism and Related Rites,* Renewing Worship, vol. 3 (Augsburg Fortress, 2002), and *Life Passages: Marriage, Healing, Funeral,* Renewing Worship, vol. 4 (Augsburg Fortress, 2002). Participants in the preparation of those provisional resources are listed in the acknowledgments sections of the volumes.

The material on pages 1-96 is covered by the copyright of this book. Unless otherwise noted, the material has been prepared by Renewing Worship editorial teams. Material from the other sources listed here or in the service music section is gratefully acknowledged and is used by permission. Every effort has been made to identify the copyright administrators for copyrighted texts and music. The publisher regrets any oversight that may have occurred and will make proper acknowledgment in future editions if correct information is brought to the publisher's attention.

Scripture quotations, unless otherwise noted, are from the New Revised Standard Version Bible © 1989 Division of Christian Education of the National Council of Churches of Christ in the United States of America. Used by permission.

Book of Common Prayer (1979) of The Episcopal Church: prayer of confession A and declaration of forgiveness B (Holy Communion)

Enriching Our Worship 1: Morning and Evening Prayer, The Great Litany, The Holy Eucharist, © 1998 The Church Pension Fund: blessing A (Holy Communion)

Lutheran Book of Worship © 1978, administered by Augsburg Fortress: texts of Kyrie litany, "This is the feast," and "Let the vineyards be fruitful"; address to parents, laying on of hands, and signing with the cross (Holy Baptism)

A New Zealand Prayer Book / He Karakia Mihinare o Aotearoa, © 1989 The Anglican Church in Aotearoa, New Zealand, and Polynesia: presentation of a candle (Holy Baptism)

Praying Together, © 1988 English Language Liturgical Consultation (ELLC): texts of Apostles Creed, Nicene Creed, great thanksgiving dialog, Lord's Prayer, "Glory to God," "Holy, holy, holy," "Lamb of God," "Now, Lord, you let your servant go"

Service music: Provisional Setting A, Joel Martinson, © 2004 Augsburg Fortress; Provisional Setting B, Marty Haugen, © 2004 Augsburg Fortress; see service music section for additional acknowledgments

With One Voice, © 1995 Augsburg Fortress: prayer of preparation for confession and prayer of confession A (Holy Communion); text and music of "Salvation belongs to our God" (Word and Thanksgiving)

Worship 99, © 1999 Evangelical Lutheran Church in America: thanksgiving for baptism (Holy Communion and Holy Baptism)

Limited permission is granted for congregations to reproduce the liturgies of Holy Communion, Word and Thanksgiving, and Holy Baptism (pp. 10–50) as well as additional service music items (with the exceptions noted below), provided that no part of the reproduction is for sale, copies are for local congregational use, and the following copyright notice appears:

> From *Renewing Worship Liturgies,* copyright © 2004, administered by Augsburg Fortress. May be reproduced by permission for use only between May 1, 2004 and December 31, 2006.

The following service music items are specifically excluded from this provision: R315, R316, R322, R329, R330, R338, R339, and R340. You must contact the copyright holder listed with each of these items (or hold a current license that covers the material) for permission to reproduce any of these service music selections.

Indexes for the Service Music

TEXT AND MUSIC SOURCES

1 John 4:12, 16 R356
Arthur, John W. R323, R324, R332, R333
Beech, Jay R357, R359
Berthier, Jacques R329
Capers, James R334
Cool, Jayne Southwick R362
Farlee, Robert Buckley R311, R355
Friesen-Carper, Dennis R334
Galatians 3:27, 29 R347, R348
Harbor, Rawn R350, R351, R366
Harling, Per R335, R336, R337
Haugen, Marty R306, R307, R308, R309, R310, R313, R321, R324, R327, R328, R333, R342, R345
Hillert, Richard R352
Hobby, Robert A. R348
Houge, Ben R356
Hurd, David R322
Jortack, Victor R343

Kolisi, G. M. R315
Lim, Swee Hong R316
Martinson, Joel R301, R302, R303, R304, R305, R312, R314, R320, R323, R325, R326, R332, R341, R344
Mummert, Mark R319, R365
Organ, Anne Krentz R353, R361
Plainsong, traditional R317, R346
Proulx, Richard R330, R338, R339, R340
Psalm 90:1 R363
Revelation 5, 19 R323, R324
Ruiz, José R354, R364
Russian Orthodox, traditional R318
Sappington, Ralph C. R331, R347
Schalk, Carl R349, R363
Schulz-Widmar, Russell R358
Schwarz, May R360
Taizé Community R329
Traditional R365, R366

TITLES AND FIRST LINES

Acclamation R304, R309, R336, R339
All of Us Go Down to the Dust R365
Alleluia R301, R306, R325, R326, R327, R329
Alleluia (Verse of the Day) R325, R327
Alleluia. Lord, to Whom Shall We Go? R306, R326
Alleluia. Your Words Are Sweet R301, R328
Amen R305, R310, R337, R340
Blessed Be God, the Source of All Life R349, R350
Blessed Be God, Who Chose You R353, R354
Blessed Be God, Who Forgives R361
Christ Has Died R304, R309, R336, R339
Cordero de Dios R343
Create in Me a Clean Heart R334
Give Rest, O Christ R364
Glory to God R320, R321, R322
Glory to You, O Word of God R330
God Is Love R356
Healer of Boundless Compassion R358, R359
Holy God R318, R319
Holy, Holy, Holy R303, R308, R335, R338
Into Paradise R366

In Peace, Let Us Pray R312, R313
Kyrie R312, R313, R314, R315, R316, R317
Lamb of God R341, R342, R343
Lenten Acclamation R302, R307, R330
Let the Vineyards Be Fruitful R332, R333
Let Your Steadfast Love R302, R307
Lord, Have Mercy R314, R315, R316, R317
May the Blessing of God R357
May the God of All Healing R362
Nkosi, Nkosi R315
Now, Lord, You Let Your Servant Go R344, R345, R346
O God, You Have Been Our Refuge R363
O Lord, Hear Our Prayer R331
Praise to the Blessed and Holy Trinity R351, R352
Salvation Belongs to Our God R311
Springs of Water, Bless the Lord R355
This Is the Feast R323, R324
Trisagion R318, R319
You Anoint My Head R360
You Belong to Christ R347, R348

To submit an evaluation for this and other Renewing Worship
provisional resources, visit the Renewing Worship Web site at
www.renewingworship.org.

ISBN 0-8066-7025-8

90000

Augsburg Fortress

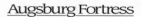

www.renewingworship.org